1 3 5 7 9 10 8 6 4 2

First published in the United Kingdom in 1999 by Ebury Press
Random House · 20 Vauxhall Bridge Road · London SW1V 2SA

Random House Australia (Pty) Limited
20 Alfred Street · Milsons Point · Sydney · New South Wales 2061 · Australia

Random House New Zealand Limited
18 Poland Road · Glenfield · Auckland 10 · New Zealand

Random House South Africa (Pty) Ltd
Endulini · 5A Jubilee Road · Parktown 2193 · South Africa

Random House UK Limited Reg. No. 954009

A CIP catalogue record for this book is available from the British Library

ISBN: 0 09 186937 4

Printed and bound by Tien Wah Press · Singapore

# To you with love

NANETTE NEWMAN

EBURY PRESS
LONDON

# Foreword

It just doesn't seem possible that it is well over twenty years ago since I had the idea of putting together a collection of children's sayings under the title *God Bless Love*. It proved a success and I followed the book with five others.

Like so many mothers I knew when my own daughters, Sarah and Emma, were young, I was often amused by things our children would come out with. We would swap sayings that had made us laugh, proudly show the latest works of artistic genius pinned to the fridge, and often be amazed at the perception in what one of our small ones had said. We would say 'I must write that down' or 'I'll always remember that', but more often than not, we didn't, and many of the sayings were lost forever or drifted away beyond memory as the children grew up.

It was this that made me decide to gather together the sayings from both family and friends' children and also spread the net wider and enlist the help of schools and

Nanette by Elizabeth          Nanette by Chris          Nanette by Caroline

hospitals. Very soon material was pouring in from all over Britain and I came to the conclusion that many people like me who love the cynical, sophisticated, send-uppish style of humour, also enjoy the very different type of humour that comes from a small child, because, in their innocence, they frequently have the knack of getting to the heart of the matter.

I was thrilled when I was approached by Ebury Press to re-publish an amalgam of those first books and I decided to add some new sayings to a selection of the old. I realise that now, with five grandchildren, I am lucky not to have lost touch with that enchanting time in a child's life when they say it like it is and 'saying it like it is' is so often worth listening to.

I hope you enjoy this collection. It comes 'To You With Love' and I am sure it will trigger off many 'you know what so and so said the other day'.

I hope so.

Nanette by Alexander          Nanette by Alice          Nanette by Emma

its apity you have To
fall in love With boys because
they all Ways pinch you

Beryl aged 7

when you marry a girl you have to
give her best man

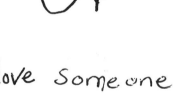

Richard aged 7

you should never love Some one
you dont like much

Katy aged 7

My Granddad says he doesnt
like women So we bought
Him a cat

Robert aged 8

To get married you have to shave you're legs. I think

Alice aged 5


I wouldn't fall in love because girls are all spotty and they Wisper

Norman aged 6


You must take care of Love — if You Don't it goez bad

James aged 5

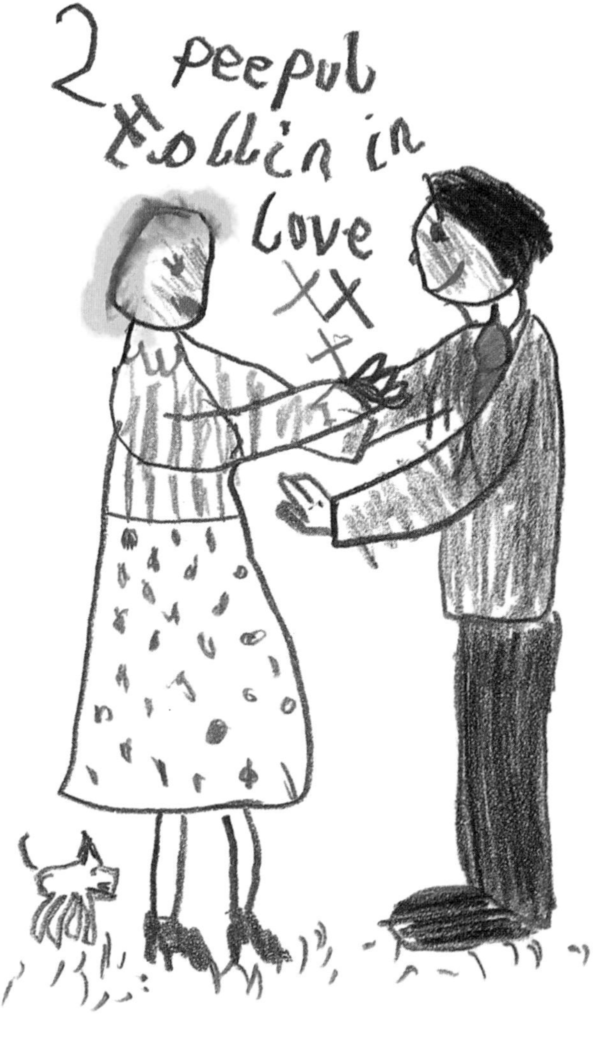
2 peepul
follin in
Love
XX
X

I saw a book once with all drawings in it about falling in love and I think you have to have eggs.

Vera aged 5

I dont like to see old ladies

and men getting married becaus theyre to old for it

Dino aged 6

It is silly to get Married before you are 12

Edward aged 6

I don't know why my
uncle wanted an awful
wedded wife

Laurie aged 7

my dad was going to marry my mum but he forgot

Nick aged 6

They throw rice pudding at you when you get married

Anya aged 5

My sister kisses her boy friend all the time its very nasty to watch

James aged 6

when I get married I'll have a cake like snow white and we'll play pass the parcel

Olivia aged 5

My mother said she won't get maried again it's too much truble

Shirley aged 5

My dad has found a better mummy for us than the last one.

Michael aged 6

I am helping my Mummy choose my next Daddy.

Anna aged 5

when You're pregnant you become
Sicker and faxter and nastier
every day

Marianne aged 9

if You put a man and a
woman in bed together
one of them will have a baby

Paul aged 9

The man next door has a
baby in his tummy but it
never comes out

Janet aged 6

i nearly know how to have babies
but we doht do it till hext term

Frances aged 7

If you dount want babies you
should practice contradiction

Lynn aged 9

To have a baby you have to make love to someone who doesn't mind

Marianne aged 9

Babies come out of your tummy on a piece of string.

Graham aged 7

A baby comes out of the mummy tummy and bites the Doctor, and the Docor smacks it.

Edward aged 6

A new borned baby can't talk it just thinks all day

Tina aged 6

Once you've had a baby you cant
it back.

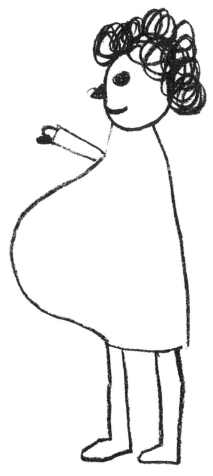

Andrea aged 6

f you dont want to have a baby you
ave to wear a safety belt

Alison aged 5

Babies cry in the Dark
becorse they thnk they
haunt been born yet.

Lorri aged 6


you        have      to      Love
    yow  loaby   brother
otherwise  ne  geas  wind

Alice aged 4


Babies are'nt Very useful

Brian aged 6

IF a baby dropz out of
your tummy when your
zhopping You must ring
the police.

Deborah aged 6

Babees need to be loved by their mother in case evrybody hates them when they grow up.

Norman aged 7

If you don't love your baby it won't come and visit you when your old

Noura aged 7

My brother was born even though I didnt want him.

Noel aged 6

my mummy let me hold my brother when he was born and I didn't drop him once

Serena aged 8

My Auntys baby jumped out of her tummy when she wasn't looking, and she hadn't bought the cot yet

Isabelle aged 6

Mum had twins my brother went up to heaven but I stayed here

Joshua aged 6

you should never squeeze a baby when
its new because its head isn't set yet

Charles aged 6

my mother has witish yeleow hare. pinkish eyes and lots of teeth and she Is very biutifull.

Anna aged 6

MY uncle has started
to grow to look
Like a mouse.

Simon aged 5

I want to Swop my Sister for Somethiing better.

Alex aged 4

We went to peter Pan and I hoped that Tinkerbell Would die because shes like my Sister.

Guy aged 6

If my sister keeps on looking in the mirrer she'll Turn into a vanity

Susan aged 6

My sister carnt reed or rite and shes a literat

Paula aged 8

Auntie Iris came all the way from Skegness.

Steven aged 6

mummy went away even though I loved her.

Michael aged 6

so me thing that makes me sad

I went on holiday to Brocolli last year

Sally aged 5

I am thankful to God for making
me only one brother and not
making me have two

Elizabeth aged 9

my sister

I was adopted so my

parents wanted me

very badly.

Lydia aged 8

We are going to
Windsor Castle to see
the Queen's private parts

Becky aged 7

# Peace

My
Peace. mummy and daddy like
They dont often get it.

David aged 7

My brothers and sisters.

David Andrew Robin Steven Caroline Kingsley Diane

True love is when some thing has died and you still remember it like my hamster.

Bobby aged 6

My rabbit is the saddest person I know.

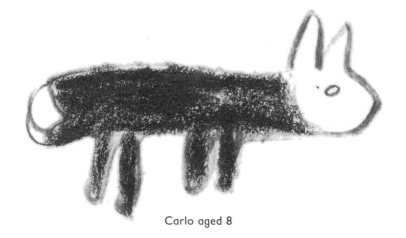

Carlo aged 8

Goldfish are sex ~~maniaks~~ mainiaks

Shaun aged 9

I would like to marry my dog.
but it isint alowed, is it?

Bruce aged 6

it is easier to have a baby if you a cat

Tricie aged 6

# Guinea Pigs Like Peace

Emma aged 4

Vanessa My Hamster

My rabbit was a be bachelor.

David aged 5

I think rabbits make very good mothers

Sara aged 6

My dog wants to give all dogs he meets babies. Hes a terrible responsiblity

Albert aged 7

I had a baby budgie called Tabatha but she died before she knew what she was.

Ruth aged 8

A ladybrd is a very cheep pet

Hugo aged 6

My rabit was very sorri to di becorse he likked eeting

Rushka aged 5

You can't teach a
goldfish anything
they're too lazy

Yasmin aged 6

My hamster went to heaven and came back a different colour.

Marilyn aged 6

My budgie broke is neck.
It served him rite because
he was always kissing himself
in the mirrer.

Tim aged 6

when I am at school
mummy
haz fun

Stephen aged 5

**Bananas are the best fruit
because you can undress them**

Yasmin aged 5

My mummy cried on my first day
at school so I had to take
her home.

Penny aged 5

My Teecher is very crule.
She smaks Peple all day
and she eets frogs legs
and maks cros spells.
I dont like her becos
she says I tell fibs.

David aged 6

I love my daddy
becorse he give
me a good ejukashun

Zoe aged 6

MY MUMMY GOZE
TO A SE2KOOL
FOR HAVING
8 bäbis

This is god

People keep their eyes open when they
pray in case Jesus arrives

Adam aged 7

Jesus had a cow and

a donkey but I think

he would rather have

had a hamster.

Brent aged 6

My sister is always writing to Jesus an he sends
her choclates an once he sent her Two lots of choclates
on the same day but she won't tell me where to write.

Ian aged 6

I say my Prayers with my
eyes open So I can hear what
I am saying.

Robin aged 5

god loves everyone who is good
like me and my friend lucy but
not peopul like gillian who takes
other peoples rubbers

Katy aged 6

I saw Jesus in the supermarket once. He was giving away soap powders

Lynne aged 6

at harvest festival God comes down and eats all the Food in the church

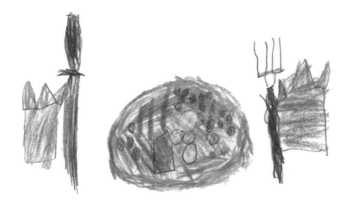

Melanie aged 5

I think  the Pope must have
been a   good baby

Elizabeth aged 6

If you eat sweets in church the vicar tells Jesus

Robert aged 5

My granny always talks to Jesus on Sundays. The rest of the week she goes to Bingo which is where he lives sometimes.

Charles aged 5

They told me to bow to the Alter but he wasnt there. I think he'd gone out with the vicar.

Emma aged 7

I think Jesus was black like me

Hamen aged 7

Salome danced naked
infront of Harrods

Annabel aged 7

Nuns have neck laces which they
Fiddle about with in church

Darin aged 8

Vicars can say Jesus Christ
but if I say it
I get a smack

Luke aged 6

The animals went into the Ark two by two
but they came out lots and lots becuase they
had some baby's during the week

Jane aged 6

when people start wars they never know how to stop.

Alanda aged 6

I think war is exciting on television for real I think It is horrible

John aged 7

Lynn aged 7

In our school Nativity play,
Joseph got chickenpox and
spoilt it

Amanda aged 7

Mary and her husband
tried to get a room at the
Holiday inn but it was full

Mark aged 7

If you are jewish you don't
have christmas you have
a harmonica instead

Edward aged 6

PEACE ON EARTH.

Father christmas
and jesus are
best friends

Darryl aged 7

Joseeph's wife Mary had an
Immaculate contraption

Cathy aged 7

Jesus was born witha yellow
frill round his head like
his mother

Jeffrey aged 5

We are doing an activity play this Christmas, it's about how Jesus was bored

Melanie aged 5

Nobody covered Jesus up When he Was born, he could have caught FLU

Sidney aged 5

people keep starring at baby Jesus because mary really wanted a girl

Kirsten aged 6

# I don't know how the King got Frankenstein into the box

Daniel aged 6